A Guide to God

What Is God Like?

Basic Bible Studies for Everyone

HARVEST HOUSE PUBLISHERS
EUGENE, OREGON

WHAT IS GOD LIKE?
Stonecroft Bible Studies
Copyright © 2012 by Stonecroft Ministries, Inc.
www.stonecroft.org
Published by Harvest House Publishers
Eugene, Oregon 97402
www.harvesthousepublishers.com

ISBN 978-0-7369-5190-6 (pbk.)
ISBN 978-0-7369-5191-3 (eBook)

Contents

Acknowledgments

Stonecroft wishes to acknowledge Janice Mayo Mathers for her dedication in serving the Lord through Stonecroft. Speaker, author, and National Board Member, Jan is the primary author of revised Stonecroft Bible Studies. We appreciate her love for God's Word and her love for people who need Him. Stonecroft also thanks the team who surrounded Jan in prayer, editing, design, and creative input to make these studies accessible to all.

Welcome to
Stonecroft Bible Studies!

At Stonecroft, we connect you with God, each other, and your communities.

It doesn't matter where you've been or what you've done... God wants to be in relationship with you. And one place He tells you about Himself is in His Word—the Bible. Whether the Bible is familiar or new to you, its contents will transform your life and bring answers to your biggest questions.

Gather with people in your community—women, men, couples, young and old alike—and explore together what God has revealed about Himself in the Bible. Find out how a God who is magnificent and powerful beyond words has expressed His love and His desire to have a relationship with each person. And find out how He has made this life-transforming friendship with us possible.

Each chapter of *What is God Like?* includes discussion questions to stir up meaningful conversation, specific Scripture verses to investigate, and time for prayer to connect with God and each other.

Discover more of God and His ways through this small-group exploration of the Bible.

Tips for Using This Study

This book has several features that make it easy to use and helpful for your life:

- The page number or numbers given after every Bible reference are keyed to the page numbers in the *Abundant Life Bible*. This handy paperback Bible uses the New Living Translation, a recent version in straightforward, up-to-date language. We encourage you to obtain a copy through your group leader or at stonecroft.org.

- Each chapter ends with a section called "Thoughts, Notes, and Prayer Requests." Use this space for notes or for thoughts that come to you during your group time or study, as well as prayer requests.

- In the back of the book you will find "Journal Pages"—a space available for writing down how the study is changing your life or any other personal thoughts, reactions, and reflections.

- Please make this book and study your own. We encourage you to use it and mark it in any way that helps you grow in your relationship with God!

If you find this study helpful, you may want to investigate other resources from Stonecroft. Please take a look at "Stonecroft Resources" in the back of the book or online at **stonecroft.org/store**.

stonecroft.org

God Is

I don't know what I believe." The young woman's eyes were dark with questions as we sipped from our steaming cups of coffee. It was clear to me that she was unable to fathom the idea that a loving God existed, let alone that God would care about her or want a personal relationship with her.

I ventured out and asked, "What if I told you that the God of the Bible wants to be your Father? How would that make you feel?"

"I'd hate it," she said without reservation.

"Why does that bother you? What is it about knowing He's a Father that's so disturbing to you?"

"Why would I want to know a God who resembles a man who was so distant, so demanding—domineering even? What kind of a God is that?"

I looked down at my coffee, mulling over her questions...internally struggling with what she had experienced. Her questions made sense to me—and they are questions that demand more than a pat answer. *How would you respond if you were part of the conversation?*

I listened. She shared how her father had been physically present in their home, but was very distant and disconnected from her. It seemed the only time he gave her any attention was when it was time to enforce discipline or set her or one of the other children straight.

I gently continued our conversation. "If you would allow me, I would like to introduce you to the God of the Bible. This true God, who calls Himself 'Father,' is very much interested in you personally. He wants a relationship with you."

There was a long silence. I waited and watched as she carefully considered the risk. I prayed in my heart, *Oh Lord, let her see you for who you really are.*

And then she spoke. "Okay, I'll do it. But you need to know that I'm not even sure what I believe, and I don't know much about the Bible."

"That's fine," I replied. "We'll learn together."

〰〰〰〰〰〰〰〰〰

This study will introduce you to God. Along with growing together in our understanding that He is a Father, we will explore other facets of who God is and what He is like. And while we can't possibly cover everything about God in one study, our desire is that together we will discover—or rediscover—who He really is.

⸺⸙⸺

Prayer

God, I want to know you, the real you. Your Word says that when I seek you, I will find you. As I begin this study, help me to seek you sincerely and intentionally. And when I experience doubt, or when my own filters get in the way, and when I have questions, help me—yes, help me with my unbelief (Matthew 7:7-8, page 738, and Mark 9:24, page 769).

Who Is God?

Who is God? This question has perplexed humanity for thousands of years. Generation after generation has searched deep into history and explored the far reaches of what is possible, hoping to unveil the ultimate answer to the existence of our universe. Everyone—even those who say they are agnostics and atheists—recognizes there is "something" that, even with our staggering accumulation of knowledge and discoveries, still cannot be explained. So the quest continues to discover the "who" or "what" behind our universe.

Human beings seem to want irrefutable proof that God exists. We want to understand how He works. And we want to know how He relates to each of us individually. This is big. It's a little like an ant trying to understand how the mind of a quantum physicist works. But the wonderful truth is, there are some things, in fact many things, we *can* understand about God because He Himself has made it possible. And exploring those things is the purpose of this study, as we

- learn what the Bible says about God
- gain a deeper understanding of His character
- develop a deeper, more meaningful relationship with Him as our Father
- discover how different and exciting life can be when we know Him intimately

Our Source About God

You may not be familiar with the Bible, and perhaps you aren't sure whether it can be trusted or whether it's relevant to us in the twenty-first century. Much could be said about these questions, and later in this chapter we will consider them more.

Briefly, however, the Bible is the most radically life-changing writing that has ever existed. It is also, by far, the most reliable ancient writing we have today. It has been investigated, tested, and trusted by countless people over the centuries.

These are just two of the reasons that many people have trusted it as God's own communication to humanity—His inspired Word, an amazing gift He has given us so we can know Him intimately and have our lives changed by our relationship with Him.

As you read the Bible, test it by asking the following questions:

1. What is it saying?

2. What does it mean?

3. What is God saying to me personally?

As you consider these questions, you'll find that the words will begin to have an impact on your life. The Bible will gain more significance for you as you begin to understand how God wants to communicate with and relate to you and everyone in the world.

God Is

When you see the statement "God is," what is the first thing that comes to your mind? Be very honest.

The very first words of the Bible are *"In the beginning God..."* There's no attempt to explain *who* God is or *that* He is. It just says, *"In the beginning God..."* In other words, God is. Read a little further down the first page of the Bible and you see that He is the One who has caused everything else to come into existence. It can't be explained in terms understandable to us, but the truth is...

> God always has been.
> God always will be.
> Therefore—*God is*.

In the New Testament, the Bible expresses the fact that "God is" in another way. Colossians 1:15-17 (page 902) tells us about Christ, who is God.

What does it say about God?

There has never been a time when God did not exist and there never will be. He simply *is*. He always *was* and always *will be*. God is present tense. God is always *now*.

God Is Eternal

The concept of eternity is ultimately impossible to grasp because we, as humans, live within the limitations of time. Everything we do is measured relative to time, so we cannot comprehend timelessness. Despite the limitations of our understanding, God is timeless.

What do the following verses say?

Nehemiah 9:5 (page 377)

Psalm 102:12,25-27 (pages 459-460)

God is always present tense. We aren't. We live in three tenses—past, present, and future. We had a beginning point in the past, we are living in the present, and our physical bodies will have an ending point in the future. The Bible tells us that God created human beings in His image, and God is eternal. Although we have a specific point at which we came into existence and have always lived within the restriction of time, there will be no ending point to our existence.

There's something else to think about, though. We tend to think of *eternal* and *eternal life* just in the sense of timelessness. But it's more. Read what Jesus says about God the Father in John 5:26 (page 813).

What do you think *"life in himself"* means?

Consider it. Can you sustain and supply your own life—body, emotions, intellect, spirit, everything that's *you*—without help? Can you do it for ever and ever? No. But God can. He has life in Himself, and He is the very Source of Life.

And here is the amazing part. God wants to share His kind of life— eternal life—with us. Go back a few verses to John 5:24 (page 813). When you believe in God, you receive eternal life now. Jesus says that those who have believed *"have already passed from death into life."*

All people will exist forever. But existing forever will be unimaginably dreadful if we are cut off from God and His life. No one needs to suffer this fate. As Jesus said, *"Those who listen to my message and believe in God who sent me have eternal life"* (John 5:24, page 813).

Some people suggest that hell is best described as an unending existence totally and finally separated from God and His light, life, and love. God forces no one to choose Him, so people can choose to remain separated from Him now and for eternity. The apostle Jude described such self-obsessed people as *"wandering stars, doomed forever to blackest darkness"* (Jude 13, page 947).

Now read John 11:25-26 (page 820). Share your thoughts about these verses.

God Is Creator

Before time began, there was nothing but God—no universe, no earth, no sun, moon, or stars—nothing. Then God began filling the emptiness, creating things out of nothing. He is the Creator of all that exists. Let's see what the Bible says about God the Creator. Read Genesis 1 (pages 3-4).

How did God create these things?

Isn't that amazing? He *spoke* things into being. All that exists around us is here because God spoke it into being. The one exception is humanity. Read Genesis 2:7 (page 4) and Genesis 1:27 (page 3).

How was the man created?

What caused the life within him?

Why do you think God spoke every aspect of creation into existence *except* human beings? What is the significance of that?

Think about how *personal* this process was. God didn't just speak the first human into being—He formed him, using *Himself* for a pattern. Not only that, He breathed the breath of life into him (Genesis 1:27, page 3, and 2:7, page 4). Do you sense the extra measure of love and creativity that went into the creation of humans? Could it be because God had something more significant planned for us?

There Is Only One God

Something else the Bible tells us about God is that He is the only true God. While there are man-invented gods, the Bible is clear when it speaks of the one true God. Read the following verses, and note what they say:

Isaiah 44:6 (page 551)

Isaiah 45:5 (page 552)

1 Corinthians 8:4-6 (page 874)

Revelation 22:13 (page 962)

These verses, and many others in the Bible, state very clearly that there is only one true God.

God Is Relational

After reading what's above, you may ask, "What does this God want with me?"

God made us so that we could know Him and have an authentic relationship with Him. Throughout the Bible, from the very beginning, God reveals Himself as in community. He describes Himself as Father, Son, and Holy Spirit. During the formation of the world and of humankind, God describes Himself as "us." Read the following passages, and note what they tell us about the nature of God.

Genesis 1:2b (page 3)

Genesis 1:26 (page 3)

John 14:7-9 (page 823)

The Bible indicates throughout that God the Father, Jesus the Son, and the Holy Spirit are one Being. We have one God who is three different Persons. They are co-equal, co-existent, and co-eternal. We often refer to all three as the Trinity.

From eternity past, the Three have been One, and the One has been Three. They exist forever in a loving, giving relationship. This information is clear in the Bible, but to a degree is not understandable to us. It is sometimes referred to as the "mystery of the Trinity." When we trust Jesus as our Savior, God gives us His Spirit to live in us, guide us, and bring us into His wonderful life of relationship.

What are you learning about God through His nature?

Through our relationship with Him, God has promised us an abundant life—a *"rich and satisfying life"* (John 10:10, page 819). One aspect of that abundance—an incredible aspect of it—is that it will continue on throughout eternity.

All of our earthly relationships will end eventually—some by choice or unavoidable circumstances, some by betrayal or abandonment, and some by death. Our relationship with God, however, will last forever. When we choose Him, no power in the universe can separate us from His love.

If you've been wounded by a past or current relationship, this might be difficult to imagine, but by the end of this study, my prayer is that you will know God and understand that He is 100 percent trustworthy. When He promises you that His love is as eternal as He is, it's true! Write down your honest thoughts and view of God.

Now, read what you just wrote and turn it into a prayer to God. Whatever you wrote, He will understand, and the more honest you are, the better. He wants to prove Himself to you.

God Relates to Us Through His Word

Why did God give us the Bible? This is a great question and warrants discussion. Depending on our view of God, we might be tempted to view the Bible as a rule book, a list of do's and don'ts. Or we might tend to think of it as a book of principles for getting what we want out of life. But the relational Father God we are learning about cannot be reduced to rules or principles. He wants a relationship with us, and the Bible is one way He communicates with us. It is filled with life-giving messages of hope, love, and faith. When we read His words in the Scriptures, we will discover more fully all that He has done for us, so that we will know Him better and better.

What is your view of the Bible today?

Is the Bible True?

You might be having questions come to mind such as "How do we know the Bible is true?" "Is there proof of its validity?" Since we've been answering all of our questions from the Bible, let's take some time to see exactly what it is. Is it a dependable, authoritative resource for our answers?

Approximately 40 different people authored the Bible, and all of them indicated that they were writing under divine inspiration—in fact, that claim is made over 3000 times in the Bible. Remarkably, these people wrote from three continents—Europe, Asia, and Africa—and their writing occurred during a span of more than 1500 years. Further, they were from widely varying socioeconomic groups and had different levels of education and different philosophical backgrounds. Finally, they wrote in three different languages—Hebrew, Aramaic, and Greek.

Even with the variety of authors and the huge span of time and distance, the Bible is in perfect harmony from beginning to end.

Although it deals with many difficult subjects, each part of the Bible is dependent on the other parts to complete the incredible story of how God provided a way for people to be reconnected with Him— all who choose to believe and receive His wonderful gift of relationship through Jesus Christ.

Prophecy Supports the Truth of the Bible

Some of the books of the Bible were written by prophets. These were people who, under God's influence, foretold coming events before they happened. The purpose of Bible prophecy is to show that God exists and that He has a plan for His creation. By foretelling events sometimes hundreds of years before they occurred, God gave us knowledge of His plan and what will happen in the future. He also shows us He can be trusted to follow through on what He promises.

The fact of fulfilled prophecy is perhaps the strongest argument for the divine inspiration of the Bible. Many prophecies in the Old Testament concern the birth, life, death, and resurrection of a man called the Messiah—God's "Chosen One." The New Testament reports in detail the fulfillment of these prophecies by Jesus Christ. We

> The word *Christ* is a Greek translation of the Hebrew word *Messiah*. Both refer to exactly the same person: God's "Anointed One" or "Chosen One."

don't have time to look at all of them, but let's look at two examples of Old Testament prophecies that were fulfilled in the New Testament.

Two Examples of Fulfilled Prophecy

The prophet Micah predicted the birthplace of Jesus 700 years before He was born. Read Micah 5:2 (page 706). What is the prophecy?

Now read Matthew 2:4-11 (page 734). Where was Jesus born?

Mary (Jesus' mother) lived in northern Israel, in a town called Nazareth in the region of Galilee, for most of her pregnancy. Bethlehem was in the region of Judea in southern Israel, near the city of Jerusalem. However, just before Jesus was born, the Roman government ordered a census to be taken for tax purposes. People were to return to the hometown of their ancestors to be registered. Joseph and Mary were from the royal line of King David, whose hometown was Bethlehem (1 Samuel 16:1, page 223). While they were there, Jesus was born, thus fulfilling the prophecy that He would be born in Bethlehem. How likely is it that the alignment of all these events is pure coincidence? Only God could have brought all those different factors together at the right time.

Another example of Old Testament prophecy being fulfilled in the New Testament has to do with King David. In his poetry, written about a thousand years before Jesus was born, he foretold numerous details of Jesus' crucifixion.* Read Psalm 22:18 (page 423). What does it say the people did?

---

* Interestingly, historical research indicates that crucifixion was unknown in David's time. It was invented hundreds of years later.

Now read John 19:23-24 (page 827). What does it say the men did?

Don't you find it amazing that a detail as small and seemingly insignificant as throwing dice played a part in a prophecy and its fulfillment? Compound that small detail with the larger detail that the prophecy was fulfilled by *Roman* soldiers, who would have known nothing about the prophetic poetry of David, a Jew from the distant past. They would never have connected their actions with the man they'd just crucified. Only God, who sees all of time from beginning to end, could have seen to it that every tiny detail was fulfilled hundreds of years later.

A Reliable Source

Jesus had something interesting to say about the Old Testament prophecies concerning Him. Read Luke 24:27,44 (page 808).

Why do you think it was necessary for every prophecy to be fulfilled?

By the time you get through all the prophecies about the Messiah, to claim that everything was a coincidence would be lunacy. And remember, Old Testament prophecy covers other events besides the birth, death, and resurrection of Jesus. The book of Daniel, for instance, prophesied the destruction of Jerusalem and the temple hundreds of years before these events occurred. Every fulfilled prophecy further confirms the Bible is a divinely inspired book.

How does knowing more about the fulfillment of prophecy impact your ability to believe that the Bible is trustworthy?

There's one more verse for us to look up about the Bible being divinely inspired by God. Read 2 Timothy 3:16-17 (page 915).

What does it say?

What are the five ways God's inspired Word can help us?

1.

2.

3.

4.

5.

There are many self-help books available for any issue we could possibly face—from drug addiction to stress and anxiety to trouble with children, and hundreds more. Some are beneficial, some aren't. Only one book has *reliable* solutions for the issues of life. It's called the Bible. Whatever kind of help you need, God, through His inspired Word, has given you every tool necessary to live an abundant, productive life.

To summarize this chapter, we've seen the following:

- God *is*. He is present tense, always now.
- He is eternal—He always has existed and always will exist.
- He is life Himself and wants to share that life with people.
- He is the Creator of everything in heaven and earth.
- He is relational. He has existed eternally as Father, Son, and Holy Spirit and wants to be in a relationship with each one of us.
- God recorded His inspired Word in the Bible.

Which of these truths do you think will make the biggest difference in the way you live your life tomorrow?

What questions do you have in relation to these statements about God?

What does the expression "God is" mean to you since you have studied this chapter?

———————— *Personal Reflection and Application* ————————

From this chapter,

I see…

I believe…

I will…

Prayer

"You are worthy, O Lord our God, to receive glory and honor and power. For you created all things, and they exist because you created what you pleased." Help me as I learn more about you (Revelation 4:11, page 952).

Thoughts, Notes, and Prayer Requests

What Is God Like?

A seven-year-old was totally engrossed in a picture he was drawing, when his mom came to look over his shoulder for a moment. "What are you drawing, Chris?" she asked.

"It's a picture of God, Mom," he replied.

"But Chris," she said, "no one knows what God looks like."

"They will when I'm done!" Chris replied.

Prayer

God, you have promised to guide me along the best pathway for my life. You have also promised to advise me and watch over me. Help me to trust you, and thank you for your unfailing love. Guide me as I learn more about you (Psalm 32:8,10, page 427).

Take a moment and make a short list of the first words that come to your mind when you think of God.

Why did you pick those words? Are they based on what you've heard or been taught, or on personal experience? Did an abundance of words come to mind, or did you struggle to come up with any words at all?

It is impossible for our finite minds to comprehend an infinite God. Our thought capacity is hopelessly inadequate. We have nothing to compare Him to, and even our *best* description is a poor expression of who He really is. Nonetheless, God is a subject about which we *cannot* be neutral. Our view of God—even if we think He doesn't exist or is irrelevant—is the most important view we will ever have, and it will affect every aspect of our life! Let's look at some of the ways that God is described in the Bible.

God Is Infinite

Infinite means God has no limitations. He does not have the same conditions of existence that we have. We need air, food, and water to exist, but God exists complete in Himself. He needs nothing other than Himself to continue His existence forever. Read the following descriptions of God and note what they say:

John 5:26 (page 813)

John 4:24 (page 812)

Revelation 1:8 (page 949)

1 Kings 8:27 (page 265)

Job 11:7-9 (page 396)

Because God is infinite, our minds will never comprehend His full scope. But the more we learn and read about Him, the more we will understand. The more we understand, the more we will realize how utterly trustworthy He is.

> Nothing limits God, but I'm so glad His love compels Him to be in relationship with us.

He Is Beyond Our Comprehension

Read and note what the following verses say about God:

Job 37:5 (page 411)

Numbers 23:19 (page 126)

Isaiah 55:8-9 (page 560)

What are your thoughts when you consider both the magnitude of God and His love for us (John 3:16, page 811)?

A passage of Scripture that beautifully sums up what we've been reading is Romans 11:33-36 (page 866). Did the last part of verse 34 make you smile? It did me, because I have to confess that I have given God much advice over the years on how He could best answer my prayers!

Just knowing all these facts about God will not necessarily change us. We need to take a step beyond pure information in order for the truth to truly impact us.

What does Psalm 145:5 (page 478) tell us to do with all of this knowledge about God?

Take a moment now and do just that. Think about the verses we've just read. What is the main thought that comes to your mind as you consider these truths about God?

God's Character Traits

You cannot trust someone until you know his or her character. What are they like? How do they react to various circumstances? The Bible tells us that God wants us to know Him, and for that reason He shows us His character throughout the Bible. Let's look at some of His character traits.

God Is Love

Think of someone you love very much. How does that love motivate you to behave?

Love seeks the best for its object, doesn't it? Love wants only good. It wants to protect and is sacrificially generous. In very simplified terms, that's how God feels about us! But His love is so much more. Love is not simply an attribute of God. God *is* love. It is His very essence. And His love cannot be corrupted by anyone or anything, the way human love can. This incomprehensible love motivates Him, it compels Him…it *is* Him. This love never fails.

The giving, self-sacrificing, unchangeable love that God has for people is not found in any other religion of the world. Love is what makes Christianity different, because God's love desires our good. God is among those who have accepted Him, loving them, enjoying them, and blessing them. Read the following verses and note what they say:

1 John 4:9-10 (page 943)

Romans 8:38-39 (page 863)

Romans 5:6-8 (page 860)

1 John 3:1a (page 942)

Which passage resonates with you the most today?

Reflecting on God's amazing love and His unending desire to connect with each of us, let's look at some other attributes of His, all of which speak of His character.

God Has All Power

God is *omnipotent*, which means He has all power. There is nothing He cannot do. Read Genesis 18:14 (page 14).

The interesting thing about this statement is the circumstances surrounding it. God had just told Sarah and Abraham, a childless couple, that they were going to have a baby. But Sarah was 90 years old! (Genesis 17:17, page 13). Nonetheless, she bore a child, just as God had said. He has the power to fulfill His promises, even when they seem impossible to people.

God Knows Absolutely Everything

God is *omniscient*, meaning that He knows absolutely everything. There is nothing He does not know. God's power and His knowledge are inseparable. Read Hebrews 4:13 (page 922), Job 28:24 (page 405), Psalm 139:1-4 (page 476), Psalm 147:5 (page 479), and Isaiah 46:9-10 (page 554).

God Is Everywhere

God is *omnipresent*. He is everywhere, all the time, at the same time. But in His "everywhere-presence," He has a special concern. Read Matthew 28:20 (page 760) and Psalm 139:7-12 (page 476).

What is God shown to care about in these passages?

Yes—His special concern is His people. That's why His omnipresence reinforces His wonderful promise: *"I will never fail you. I will never abandon you"* (Hebrews 13:5b, page 928).

God Is Faithful

When we explore how faithful God is, we begin to grasp how committed, steadfast, and unwavering He is toward us. In His faithfulness, we actually see the oneness—the unity—of all His character traits. And taken as a whole, His traits reveal His perfection.

> Rather than viewing God's omnipresence as "God is everywhere," we should view God's omnipresence as "everything is and remains in His presence." It is really awesome to consider!

Because God forever is who He is, because of His interwoven traits and attributes, He can never stop being faithful. It's simply what He is. Are you catching how complex and wonderful God is? He can't stop being faithful to who He is, because *He is*!

Once we truly start to grasp this truth, God's faithfulness in His relationship with us—His dependability, loyalty, and steadfastness—will introduce us to a level of security we never imagined. We can live with hope and anticipation for the future, because His faithfulness never fails. He keeps His promises! Read the following verses and note which of God's character traits are mentioned:

Psalm 86:15 (page 453)

1 Corinthians 1:8-9 (page 870)

2 Timothy 2:13 (page 914)

Did you notice that every character trait those verses mention involves God's loving relationship with us? He is completely faithful to stand by us and follow through on what He says!

Read Psalm 92:1-2 (page 456).

"When I think of God's faithfulness, I must include His longsuffering, His patience with each one of us. And when I think of this, I am so thankful. (He is slow to anger—not willing that any would perish.) That is amazing!"

—Cheryl Lee Davis

One of the most personal ways to understand God's faithfulness is through experiencing it in your everyday life. Share an example of a time when God's faithfulness was evident to you.

God Does Not Change

One of God's most reassuring attributes is that He is immutable. He does not change. Nothing in Him, nothing about Him will ever change. For example, God cannot be unfaithful because that would require Him to change. Read the following verses:

Malachi 3:6 (page 729)

1 Samuel 15:29 (page 222)

What is the significance of God's inability to change His mind?

God Is Good

Everyone has experienced the feeling of "being good" at some time, but divine goodness is different than human goodness. We feel good about one aspect of our life, or one thing we do quite well. But

God Himself is the measure and definition of *good*. He shows His goodness in everything He does as He simply acts like Himself, and He is *perfectly* good in all ways, at all times. In Matthew 19:17 (page 750) Jesus says, *"There is only One who is good."*

What does Psalm 107:1 (page 463) say?

Now read Psalm 31:19 (page 427).
How do you experience God's goodness in your life?

God Is Just

When God acts justly, He is not doing it to conform to what we have determined to be a just action. He is just—He is always completely just and can never be anything other than that. Read Deuteronomy 32:3-4 (page 164) and 1 John 1:9 (page 941).

What do these verses say about God?

What combination of God's traits did you notice in these two passages?

God Is Merciful

Mercifulness is not a temporary mood with God. It is one of His eternal, unchanging character traits. God was merciful before time began, and His mercy will extend through all eternity.

When we think about justice and mercy, it seems as if they conflict with each other. Humanly speaking, these traits are often exclusive. How can we be both just and merciful to all parties involved? If someone commits murder and is sentenced to life in prison, that is justice for that person, but where is the mercy? If the person is given mercy and receives a pardon, where is the justice for the victim's family?

While it's a puzzle for us, it's not with God. God is 100 percent just, and He is 100 percent merciful—at all times and in all circumstances. Only a sovereign, loving, relational God, whose very character is justice and mercy, can combine those two attributes in complete harmony. Read 2 Corinthians 1:3 (page 882).

What does it mean to you when you see that God is called a *"merciful Father"*?

God Is Holy

Holy is not a word we hear very much today (except in exclamations and expletives). The basic thought it communicates is that something or someone is set apart because of some special quality, or is devoted to some special purpose.

God stands completely apart from us in His purity and absolute moral perfection. His holiness is unique, unapproachable, and unattainable. Read 1 Samuel 2:2 (page 212) and Psalm 99:9 (page 459) to see what the Bible says about our holy God.

Are you starting to wonder how a God who is holy can also be a relational God? How could we possibly be in close relationship with Him? Now read 1 Peter 1:13-16 (page 934).

> What does this verse say about us regarding this character trait of God?

But how can we, who have sinned and disobeyed God again and again, possibly be holy? God has an answer. Read 1 Corinthians 1:30 (pages 870-871).

> How are we made holy?

Don't you find that incredible? Because of Jesus, we are holy in God's eyes! That is how much He loves us! What is your response to this?

God's answer to the "holiness problem" is so important to understand! Otherwise we will be tempted to believe that He rejects us or shuns us every time we sin.

Let's look at a fuller explanation of God's solution to the problem. The writer of the book of Hebrews reveals that *"God's will was for us to be made holy by the sacrifice of the body of Jesus Christ, once for all time"* (Hebrews 10:10, page 925). Read Hebrews 10:12-14 (page 925), which tells us what Jesus, our High Priest, has done.

What do you think *"good for all time"* means?

How many sacrifices were necessary to take care of the "holiness problem" forever?

That is how perfect, powerful, and complete Jesus' sacrifice on the cross was for us! And now *"we can boldly enter heaven's Most Holy Place because of the blood of Jesus."* Read Hebrews 10:19 (page 926).

God has taken care of the sin problem and sin question forever by the one-time sacrifice of His Son, Jesus Christ, our High Priest. The God we could not approach because of our sin is now accessible. He welcomes into His holy presence those of us who have accepted His Son's sacrifice, because we have been made holy. And we can take no credit for it. It is all His doing—the gift of His love.

Don't you sit back in awe when you think about who God is and what He is like? It makes me so thankful that He—the magnificent, all-powerful, all-holy God who fills the universe—has made a way for us to be His intimate friends. There are two powerful verses in the ninth chapter of Jeremiah that show us what our response should be in regard to who God is and all we receive from Him.

> *This is what the LORD says: "Don't let the wise boast in their wisdom, or the powerful boast in their power, or the rich boast in their riches. But those who wish to boast should boast in this alone: that they truly know me and understand that I am the LORD who demonstrates unfailing love and who brings justice and righteousness to the earth, and that I delight in these things. I, the LORD, have spoken!"* (Jeremiah 9:23-24, page 580).

Only God is worthy of praise because everything we have and are and will be is from Him. He is the one who, in His unfailing love for us, made it possible to have a personal relationship with Him.

Before we end this chapter, let's go back to the little boy we read about at the beginning who was drawing a picture of God. Let's do what he did. But instead of crayons, use words to draw a picture of what God looks like to you right now:

Personal Reflection and Application

From this chapter,

I see...

I believe...

I will...

Almighty God, thank you for revealing yourself to me through the Bible. I will praise you because your unfailing love is better than life itself. I will praise you as long as I live, lifting my hands up to you in prayer (Psalm 63:3, page 441).

Thoughts, Notes, and Prayer Requests

3

Where Is God?

Prayer

Father God, you are always near. Even when I am afraid, you make me strong and courageous. I will not panic, because you are everywhere and have said you will personally go ahead of me. You have promised you will neither fail me nor abandon me (Deuteronomy 31:6, page 163).

In this chapter, we are going to look at how the Bible answers the question "Where is God?" Look up the following verses, and note the answer next to the reference:

Psalm 103:19 (page 460)

Acts 17:24-25 (page 846)

1 Kings 8:27 (page 265)

1 Timothy 6:16 (page 913)

Jeremiah 23:23-24 (page 592)

God is always with us, but that does not always mean that we recognize Him. On the other hand, there are those times when we need to feel and know that God is with us. Consider the following verses:

Psalm 34:18 (page 428)

Psalm 145:18 (page 479)

Isaiah 43:2 (page 550)

How will God's presence with you affect how you go through various life circumstances?

Did you notice how these verses addressed both the physical and emotional aspect of where God is? Not only is He in heaven and on earth, but He is near to the brokenhearted, and all who call out to

Him. God is wherever He knows we need Him at all times. He is everywhere!

Now read 1 John 4:12 (page 943) to see what it says.

Think about that for a minute. If we love each other, God lives in us and His love is brought to *full expression* in us. How do you imagine that would look in your life? Think of a time when you felt God's love from someone else.

This is the wonderful thing: We don't have to just *imagine* God's love being expressed through our lives—we can experience it! When we love others, we open the door to the full expression of His love.

God Is Reaching Out to Us Everywhere

God wants us to know Him personally. He wants to reveal Himself to each of us, and He has made His existence clear.

How does Romans 2:14-15 (page 858) say He has done this?

God makes His existence clear in another way as well. What does it say in Romans 1:20 (page 857)?

Isn't it interesting that once again we see God revealing Himself to us both emotionally (through our conscience) and physically (through nature)? Or we could say that He reveals Himself to us both invisibly and visibly. He wants us to know Him, and He reaches out to us from all directions.

Sadly, some people persist in ignoring God. They turn their backs on the obvious—with devastating results. Read Romans 1:21-22 (page 857).

What is your reaction to this? How would you describe this passage in your own words?

God has made the fact of His existence inescapable. He has placed it around us, and He has placed it within us. Even if we refuse to acknowledge Him, there is still something within us that demands explanation. People have gone to great lengths to explain what cannot be explained except by acknowledging God, and the result of their "wisdom" is foolishness. When conclusions are drawn or decisions made on a foolish premise, chaos and conflict result.

God with Us and in Us

One of the attributes of God we discussed in the previous chapter is His omnipresence. *Omni* means "all," so *omnipresent* means God is "all-present"—present everywhere. He is not bound by space. God, in the totality of His being—without being divided, multiplied, or diffused—penetrates and fills the entire universe. This means He is present with us in real and practical ways. Note what the following verse says:

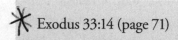 Exodus 33:14 (page 71)

Don't you love the word *"personally"* used here? Have you ever experienced God going with you someplace? What did it feel like?

Read the following verses:

Psalm 16:11 (page 420)

Psalm 31:20 (page 427)

Psalm 46:1 (page 434)

Psalm 139:7-12 (page 476)

What is the main point of these passages?

Did one verse speak very clearly to your heart? Why?

That is one way God speaks to you! He is a very personal God. Psalm 139:3 (page 476) says He knows all about you. Another translation says He is "intimately acquainted" (NASB) with all your ways. God knew you needed to read that verse on this very day—and He made sure you saw it. That is how much God loves you!

God wants to be with us. This is so wonderfully expressed in the passages we just read. But His plan is even more marvelous—He wants to make His home *inside* us! When we believe that Jesus' death on the cross is the full payment for our sins, God forgives us and makes us acceptable to Him. (We discussed how He makes us holy in the previous chapter.) At that moment, He puts Himself—the Holy Spirit—into our lives.

The study *Who Is the Holy Spirit?* can make a wonderful follow-up to *What Is God Like?* For more information, see "Stonecroft Resources" in the back of this book.

From that point on, He is always in us, and we have His companionship and guidance every day, forever. Read John 14:16 (page 823). As we practice being aware of the presence of the Holy Spirit in us moment by moment, our life will reveal a whole new meaning and purpose. We will see evidence of God working in us.

Let's look at one more passage before we move on. What does John 14:1-3 (page 823) tell us?

God not only wants to be with us and in us while we are on earth, but He is preparing a place where we can be together throughout eternity! Let that sink in for a moment, and then write out your thoughts.

God's Single Limitation

Through these verses (and there are many more besides), we have seen that God is literally everywhere. He has no limitations except for one—and that limitation He has put on Himself. He will not enter anyone's life—unless that person asks Him to.

When God created the first man, He breathed eternal life—His own life—into Adam and he became a living person. This made humans different from all the rest of His creation. God's plan has always been that we would live with Him forever. But God gave us a free will, the power of choice—which means we can choose our own destiny here on earth and for eternity. Adam and Eve, the first humans God created, chose to disobey God, and the consequence was death— separation from God. Read Romans 5:12 (page 860).

Even though Adam and Eve disobeyed, this did not change God's plan. God had already provided a way for disobedience to be forgiven. Go down a few verses and read Romans 5:15-16 (page 860). When we believe and accept Jesus Christ, who is God's provision for our sin, we will live forever in unity with Him in the place He is preparing for us. Read 1 John 5:11-12 (page 943).

This merciful action on God's part reveals even more about His character. He loves His creation, and in mercy He has graciously provided a way our relationship with Him can be restored. Our choice to yield to God or not, to be in relationship with Him or not, is the most important choice we'll ever make. One choice results in eternal life—life with Him and in Him, now and forever. One results in death—existence apart from Him, now and forever.

God created us to fully enjoy His friendship forever. We must decide whether we will live in relationship with Him or separated from Him. If you haven't yet made the decision to ask God into your life, you can do it right now. Just tell God you are ready to choose Him. Acknowledge that you sin and that God's Son, Jesus, paid the price for your sins by dying on the cross. Thank Jesus for making a relationship with God possible, and ask Him to help you follow in His footsteps.

This is such an important decision! Don't take it lightly. Share what you've done with a friend. The Bible is one of the primary ways God has chosen to speak to His children. I encourage you to start reading it regularly, so that you can build your relationship with Him.

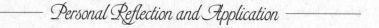

——————— *Personal Reflection and Application* ———————

From this chapter,

I see...

I believe...

I will...

Prayer

Father God, how wonderful to know that I can never leave your Spirit, your presence is all around me. Even surrounded in darkness, your light will find me. This knowledge is too wonderful for me and I praise you for it! (Psalm 139:5-12, page 476).

Thoughts, Notes, and Prayer Requests

_____

_____

_____

_____

_____

_____

_____

_____

_____

_____

_____

_____

_____

_____

_____

_____

_____

4

Does God Know Me?

When my son was in seventh grade, he brought home a report card with a failing grade on it. I was dumbfounded. Although I saw his teacher several times a week in my capacity as a parent volunteer, she'd never indicated there were problems. When I met with her to see what had happened, she looked at me sheepishly. "To tell you the truth," she admitted, "I didn't realize he was doing so poorly until I tallied up his grades. I guess he just kind of fell through the cracks."

It happens all the time. People fall through the cracks. They go unnoticed or get forgotten, and sometimes, when they finally come to someone's attention, it's too late to help. But here is an eternal truth: *You will never fall through the cracks with God!* It is impossible. You are always on His mind and in His heart. You are His beloved child.

Prayer

Lord, I will listen to you, the One who created me. I will not be afraid, for you have ransomed me and called me by name, and I am yours (Isaiah 43:1, page 550).

How Well Does God Know You?

God knows you better than you know yourself. He knows you better than anyone else knows you. It takes time to get to know another person, but God didn't need time to get to know you. He knew you before you were even conceived. In fact, He knew you before time began.

This is how much God knows you: Even before He laid out the foundations of the earth, you were in His mind. He already knew what color of eyes and hair you would have. He knew how tall you'd be and the precise pitch of your voice. He knew exactly what shade of white your teeth would have and what the circumference of your big toe would be. He also knew how sensitive you'd be, how adventurous, how intelligent. And when He worked out the millions of unique details that only you can claim, He designed a plan for your life. It's a plan that fits perfectly with your physical and emotional makeup, and God's intent is that you will impact your sphere of influence like no other person could ever do.

How Does God Feel About You?

God has always known you. Even better, He has always loved you. And because He knows and loves you more than you can possibly imagine, He has made plans for you, even a place for you, to be intimately connected with Him. This loving Father sees you as His child and wants the very best for you. Yes, our God has good in mind for you.

What do the following verses have to say about you and God?

Romans 8:38-39 (page 863)

Romans 8:29 (page 863)

John 6:37 (page 814)

Hebrews 13:5 (page 928)

Did you notice that the last verse connected finances to God's promise of provision? So often peace of mind and having money become synonymous in our minds, but God says not to go there. He is not going to abandon us. Period.

Look at the verse following this one—it's a remarkable thought. "*The LORD is my helper,*" it says, "*so I will have no fear. What can mere people do to me?*" (Hebrews 13:6, page 928). God excels at putting things in proper perspective, doesn't He? Mere human or Sovereign God—whose side do you prefer to be on?

Jesus tells a beautiful parable in Luke to illustrate how God feels about us. Read Luke 15:3-7 (pages 797-798).

One out of a hundred! That is keeping a close watch! Do you get an image of God hovering over all His creation, watching over each person? Consider the next images you see portrayed in this parable. How do you experience Jesus carrying you?

Don't you love the idea of God rejoicing over you? Every single person is of immeasurable value to God. He does not want a single one to wander away from Him. How does knowing that God rejoices over you affect the way you view Him?

Let's look at some other things God has done for us. Read Ephesians 1:3-8 (page 895) and list what it says He has done.

Quite a list, isn't it? Did you notice some of the wording used in this passage? *Every* spiritual blessing, *great* pleasure, *showered* His kindness…Everything about God is magnified beyond our comprehension—especially His love for us.

The list you just made has to do with the ways God loves you. Now read Psalm 139:1-18 (page 476) and make a list of the ways He *knows* you.

It really is amazing, isn't it? Did you love the last sentence of the passage? *"And when I wake up, you are still with me!"* How does this entire passage impact your perspective on God's omniscience?

This psalm ends with a significant prayer. Read Psalm 139:23-24 (page 477) and then rewrite the prayer in your own words. Tell God exactly what's on your heart as a result of what you've been reading.

God Knows What We Need

Even knowing how loved we are by God, even knowing how intimately He knows us, it is still so easy to get focused on all the needs and concerns of daily life. God understands that about us and has addressed those issues. Read the following verses, and note what they say:

Matthew 6:25-34 (pages 737-738)

1 Peter 5:7 (page 937)

Matthew 6:7-8 (page 737)

How would you summarize these verses?

Is there an area God has not addressed concerning the things you worry about?

Is there something you're worrying about right now? Take a moment and write a short prayer about it.

Now take it to the Lord and ask that He help you trust Him and not worry about it. *"Give all your worries and cares to God, for he cares about you"* (1 Peter 5:7, page 937).

If God already knows what we need, why do we even need to pray? It's because God wants to be in relationship with us, and relationships are two-way. They require communication. When we pray, it shifts our focus to God. It reminds us that His life is our life, and we depend on Him to supply our needs. His response renews our confidence that He is listening to us.

When we talk to the God of all power, wisdom, and love, He reminds us of His power at work in our lives; He makes His wisdom available to us and binds our heart to His. The more we talk to Him and read His words in the Bible, the more intimate our relationship with Him will be. The more intimate we become with Him, the more able we will be to trust Him no matter what comes into our lives.

God's Love for Us Is Indestructible

In the same way that God has been in every moment of our past and even before, He is in every moment of our future. We don't need to fear what the future holds because He is already there. We can be assured that whatever comes into our lives, He will not abandon us. Even more reassuring, He has promised to bring purpose to all of our circumstances.

What does Romans 8:28 (page 863) say?

Now skip down a few verses to 31-37 (page 863). Look at the list of questions it asks:

- If God is for us, who can be against us?

- Who dares accuse us?

- Who condemns us?

- Can anything separate us from Christ's love?

- Does it mean He no longer loves us if something terrible happens?

It's a magnificent list of questions with even more magnificent answers. No one! No one! No one! Nothing! No! Every answer is a resounding *no!* Only one question is answered with an affirmative: *"Since he did not spare even his own Son but gave him up for us all, won't he also give us everything else?"* Yes! God showers blessings on those who are in relationship with Him.

What a true perspective this gives us—and to know that *overwhelming* victory is ours! Take just a moment and acknowledge the immeasurable love God has for you. Write out your thoughts.

And just in case you still have a few niggling doubts about the indestructibility of God's love for you, read the final two verses of this chapter, verses 38-39 (page 863).

Did He leave anything out? Did He forget to mention the one thing that might be able to separate us from His love? *No! Because nothing can.*

God Has Made It All Possible

Before we end this chapter, let's briefly look at some of the things God does for us. As we said earlier, relationship is a two-way street. It requires participation by both parties in order to grow, flourish, and deepen. Read each verse and note what you do and what God does.

Psalm 37:4-5 (page 429)

My part:

God's part:

Proverbs 3:5-6 (page 482)

My part:

God's part:

Take another look at the verbs used in these passages to describe our participation: *Take delight, commit, trust; trust, do not depend on your own, seek.* Doesn't it seem as though our part is to rest in and enjoy what God has provided to us? Read Romans 5:9-11 (page 860). What does this say about our relationship with God?

Think of everything God has done to make our friendship with Him possible! Now the almighty God of the universe considers us His friend—a friend He would literally do *anything* for—a friend for whom He has already given the life of His dear Son! Yes, relationship is a two-way street, but in the case of God's relationship with us, He is the only reason our relationship can even exist. He has accounted for every possible barrier, hindrance, or interference between us, and now He stands in front of us with His arms open wide. It truly is an incomprehensible love, isn't it?

————— *Personal Reflection and Application* —————

From this chapter,

I see...

I believe...

I will...

Prayer

God, let me experience Christ making His home in my heart as I trust in Him. Let my roots grow down into your love and keep me strong. Give me the power to understand how wide, how long, how high, and how deep your love for me is. May I experience the love of Christ, though it is too great to fully understand. Let it make me complete with all the fullness of life and power that comes from you (Ephesians 3:17-19, page 896).

Thoughts, Notes, and Prayer Requests

_____

_____

_____

_____

_____

_____

_____

_____

_____

_____

_____

_____

_____

_____

_____

_____

_____

How Can I Get to Know God Better?

I was at a party when some friends stopped by. One young woman hovered on the edge of the crowd, speaking only when spoken to. I introduced myself but found her very reserved. She would only give me her first name and was obviously uncomfortable with my attention. I struggled to maintain the conversation and felt great relief when someone called her away.

Later in the evening, after the young woman had left, my friend asked if I knew her. "No," I said. "And she didn't make it easy to get to know her. I've never met anyone so reserved. She hardly talked at all." My friend shook her head sadly. "That's not how she is, really. She's just going through an awful time."

Events in her family had caused a once outgoing, sociable young woman to become withdrawn.

And while I'd formed an entirely incorrect opinion of her, I'm confident of God's knowledge of and love for her right where she is.

Prayer

Thank you, God, for making yourself known. Please help me to *know* you better. Give me your spiritual wisdom and understanding, so that the way I live will always honor and please you. Let my life produce every kind of good fruit, as I grow and learn to know you better and better (Colossians 1:9-10, page 902).

You can know *about* someone and still not know him or her well at all. Conclusions we draw from limited knowledge are always one-dimensional. Not until you have devoted the time to build a relationship will the various dimensions of someone's personality be revealed in a way that allows you to actually *know* them.

Starting the Relationship

Of course, before a relationship can be built, it has to be started in the first place. Through all of time, people have refused a relationship with God because they have formed wrong opinions of Him based on limited knowledge. They assume He doesn't care about them personally, or that He is far removed from humanity, or that He doesn't exist.

But God reveals Himself to humanity every day. His desire is to be known by people and for people to know Him. How do the following verses speak about His making Himself known?

Psalm 8:3-4 (page 417)

Genesis 1:27 (page 3)

2 Corinthians 4:3-4 (page 883)

But just knowing facts about God doesn't mean you know Him. A relationship built only on facts isn't a relationship. Relationship involves belief and trust, emotion and commitment, as well as knowledge. And God wants us to have a deep, abiding relationship with Him. He is the One who initiates it. It is His love that pursues; He is the One who continues to chase after us—to the point of complete sacrifice, the life of His Son. From the very beginning, God designed His creation to be in relationship with Him. He created you and me in His image. He created a place and a way for us to live in close connection with Him. That is His desire. What is your choice?

Growing Deeper in Knowing God

God is not content to simply *start* a relationship with us. He always continues to reveal Himself more. He continues to pursue us, wanting us to know Him more deeply. Read the following passages and note what they say about His revealing, pursuing love and how it is working in us.

Ephesians 2:4-10 (pages 895-896)

2 Corinthians 5:17-21 (page 884)

Romans 8:39 (page 863)

The more time you invest in a relationship, the more multidimensional it will be, the more satisfying and fulfilling—and the more beneficial. If you want to *know* God, you need to invest time in building that relationship.

Let's look as some other things the Bible says about how we can know God more deeply. Read Psalm 46:10a (page 434).

Now read the entire psalm. Considering what was happening in this passage, what does *"be still"* mean to you?

Read Hebrews 10:19-22 (page 926). Why is it that your heart can be calm and still in God's presence?

You can always have complete calm and confidence in approaching God. So don't let fear keep you away.

Staying Close to Him

Knowing God takes time, but the more time you invest, the more intimate your relationship will be. A relationship with Him also takes action. If you just read *about* Him in your Bible, all you're doing is collecting facts—and sadly, you might miss the intimacy that comes from truly knowing Him. The deep friendship He offers is too good to miss by refusing to do what He asks in His Word. The closer you follow God, the easier it will be. Remember, now that you have His life in you through the Holy Spirit, it becomes more and more natural to want to listen to Him and follow through on what He says.

I have a friend who likens her relationship with God to maintaining her goal weight. The closer you stay to your goal weight, the easier it is to maintain. If you gain a couple of pounds, it takes almost no effort to get it off. If you gain ten or fifteen pounds, it takes a little effort but it's still not too difficult. However, the farther away from your goal weight you get, the harder you have to work and the more impossible it seems to get back to where you need to be for your health and well-being. In fact, you can get so far from your goal weight you might be tempted to give up.

In some respects, fostering your relationship with God is like maintaining your goal weight. Of course, you can never actually depart from God in the way you can depart from your goal weight. Still, it is easier to hear His voice and sense His presence the more closely you stay connected with Him.

When you allow a feeling of distance to develop in your relationship with Him—through busyness, discouragement, or disobedience—His voice can be less distinct, and His presence may be not as discernible. If you do not humble yourself and acknowledge your need for Him, you will feel as if you are walking farther away from Him. The distractions could become more appealing, and your desire to listen

"If we confess our sins to him, he is faithful and just to forgive us our sins and to cleanse us from all wickedness" (1 John 1:9, page 941). The New Testament was written in Greek, and the word translated into English as *confess* could be literally translated *"to say the same thing."* In other words, confession is simply agreeing with God in regard to what He says about our sin.

to Him will be weaker. You could begin to rationalize your behavior, and every decision can reinforce the pattern until you no longer clearly hear His voice because you no longer are listening for it.

God never moves away from us. We are the ones who allow the sense of distance to come between us. We forget that His yoke is easy to bear and the burden He gives us is light (Matthew 11:28-30, page 742). He is gentle and humble at heart, always willing to hear when we acknowledge our fault. And then we can once more experience the ease of His relationship with us.

The Starting Point

Earlier in this chapter we talked about starting a relationship with God. Who exactly does He want to have a relationship with? Let's see what the Bible says about that. Read the following verses and note what they say:

1 Timothy 2:1-4 (page 910)

2 Peter 3:9 (page 939)

2 Corinthians 5:18-19 (page 884)

Matthew 11:28 (page 742)

Romans 5:8-10 (page 860)

What conclusion can be drawn from these verses?

In every relationship, there is a starting point, isn't there? You have to meet the person before you can get to know them. According to John 14:6 (page 823), how can we meet God?

The only way to truly know God is through Jesus. He is the *way* to God. He is the *truth* of God and about God. He is the very *life* of God in those who receive Him. In Jesus, *everything is covered*! If we know Jesus, we know what God is like because Jesus is the exact expression of the invisible God.

The Difference Between Knowing About God and Trusting in Him

In 1 John 1:5-10 (page 941) the apostle John passes on Jesus' message. John not only gives us a description of God, but he also talks about the difference between knowing Him and just knowing *about* Him.

What does he say God is?

When are we lying to ourselves and others?

If we only know *about* God, we are living in spiritual darkness and we are self-deceived. A head stuffed full of knowledge will do us no good. God want us to *know* Him and be in fellowship with Him. The only way this is possible is if we are cleansed from sin by the blood of Jesus.

If we only know *about* God, we have a faulty view of ourselves. What does verse 8 say that faulty view is?

What is the implication of claiming we have not sinned?

We read about this next truth in verse 9 from 1 John 5, but let's read it in Romans 3:22-25a (page 859).

The word *believe* means more than just being aware of the fact that Jesus is God's Son who died on the cross for your sins. *Believe* means to put all of your trust in Jesus. This kind of trust will always involve repenting, because to *repent* means to totally change your mind on how you view life—to change the direction you are going, to turn around. To trust Jesus with your life means you will not go your own way any longer, but that you will go God's way instead.

Being a "good person," doing more good than bad, does not earn you favor with God. It is not a matter of what you do, but who you are connected with. If you do not have God's gift of life through Christ, you are spiritually dead—separated from God. Read Ephesians 2:4-10 (pages 895-896).

What does verse 5 say about people's condition without Christ?

What did God do to help people, and why did He do it?

How do verses 6 and 7 describe those who have been raised from the dead with Christ?

What does verse 9 say about good things people do?

Who we know is the key to receiving God's life and spending forever with Him, now and in heaven. There is only one Person through whom we can be made alive.

What does it say in John 3:35-36 (page 811)?

> *God loved the world so much that he gave his one and only Son, so that everyone who believes in him will not perish but have eternal life. God sent his Son into the world not to judge the world, but to save the world through him. There is no judgment against anyone who believes in him. But anyone who does not believe in him has already been judged for not believing in God's one and only Son.*

—John 3:16-18 (page 811)

Jesus is the only way!

Have You Received God's Gift of Salvation?

If you have never received God's gift of forgiveness and promise of new life with Him, this is a great time to do it. Take some time right now and talk to God. Imagine He is visibly sitting beside you, and tell Him that you do believe Jesus is His Son and that He died to pay the price for your sins and remove the barrier between you and God the Father. Ask Him to forgive your sins and come into your life. Finally, thank God for answering your prayer. If you'd like, write your prayer out.

Some wonderful things happened when you just prayed. Read the following verses and note what they say.

2 Corinthians 5:17-18a (page 884)

John 3:36a (page 811)

Romans 5:1 (page 860)

Ephesians 1:13b-14 (page 895)

Look at what God has brought into your life by this decision: a brand-new you; eternal life—His very life; forgiveness; peace with Him; and God the Holy Spirit living in you, who is God's guarantee that you are His! Isn't that amazing? And that's not all.

Other verses tell us that when we put our faith in God, we actually become His children. Read John 1:12 (page 809) and Romans 8:15-17 (page 862).

Think about what this actually means. What does a parent–child relationship involve?

Now think about this. Even the healthiest parent–child relationships among humans have faults. With the best of intentions, the most loving and concerned parents on this planet still make mistakes with their children. *God cannot make mistakes.* His love and care for you will be without fault.

If you were to describe the perfect parent, what attributes would he or she have?

Whatever you wrote down, no matter how complete your list seems, God as your Father will be all that and more. He will be faithful in His love and care for you, generous and thoughtful, intensely interested in all you do, and pleased with your obedience. He will not abandon you, no matter what you do or think. He will be delighted by your individuality, skillful in training you, wise in guiding you—and most wonderful of all—*always* available!

IIIIIIIIIIIIIIIIIIIIIII

One last thing…now that you have a new relationship with God as your Father, you also have a new relationship with other believers. They are now your spiritual sisters and brothers—you are all heirs together with Jesus of all that God has in store for those He loves. Welcome into God's family!

> If you've been in relationship with God for some time, how do you see your relationship with Him being strengthened daily?

―――――― *Personal Reflection and Application* ――――――

From this chapter,

I see…

I believe…

I will…

Prayer

God, because I am your child, I will trust in you with all my heart and not depend on my own understanding. I will follow you in all I do and trust you to show me which path to take (John 1:12, page 809, and Proverbs 3:5-6, page 482).

Thoughts, Notes, and Prayer Requests

_____

_____

_____

_____

_____

_____

_____

_____

_____

_____

_____

_____

_____

_____

_____

6

How Can I Love God Back?

I still don't know whether or not I believe in God."

My friend and I were sharing another cup of coffee and engaging in our frequent topic of conversation: God. She still has questions; she is still longing for something more concrete, less based on trust. But her heart is beginning to open, and God does not ignore an open heart.

"But if I did believe in Him," she continued, "I think I know what He'd say to me."

"What is that?" I asked.

"He'd say, 'I am your Father, and I am right here. I love you, and I've already forgiven you.'"

I smiled. *She is exactly right!*

Prayer

Father, thank you for loving me unconditionally, forgiving all my sins, and raising me to new life in Christ. Help me to love you, walk in all your ways, obey your commands, hold firmly to you, and serve you with all my heart and all my soul (Ephesians 2:4-5, page 895, and Joshua 22:5, page 184).

God Revealed

God is revealing Himself more and more to my friend, and she is beginning to take a closer look at Him. She is sensing His love, His provision of forgiveness, and His desire to be deeply, faithfully related to her. Read Matthew 7:7-8 (page 738).

What promise do we have in seeking to know God more?

There's another passage that talks about the things God reveals to us. The apostle Paul tells us about God's "secret plan" that has now been revealed because of the death of Christ. Read 1 Corinthians 2:9-12 (page 871). In verse 9, there is a reference to the words of the Old Testament prophet Isaiah, which indicates that there was a time when God had not yet revealed His plan.

What does verse 10 tell us about the things that used to be concealed? How have we come to know them?

Why have we been given God's Spirit?

Take a moment and list a few of the wonderful things that God has freely given us.

Since God has given us so much, wouldn't it be a terrible loss to not pay attention to those things? Let's make sure we keep listening to the Spirit in us!

God Shows Us How to Know Him

God reveals Himself to us because He desires us to be intimately acquainted with Him. Discover five different ways God helps us get to know Him. Write next to each passage the way God reveals Himself to His people.

John 1:17-18 (page 809)

Romans 1:20 (page 857)

2 Peter 1:20-21 (page 938)

Acts 1:8 (page 830)

1 Timothy 1:19 (page 910)

Can you think of a specific example of God revealing Himself to you that's associated with each of these ways? If so, make note of it by each reference.

God wants us to live our life according to the purpose He designed for us. That's one reason He so readily reveals Himself to us. And as we've already noted, God has attributes that are unique to Him (that we don't share), and He uses them to reveal Himself. Because He is *omnipotent* (all-powerful), *omnipresent* (present everywhere), *omniscient* (all-knowing), *self-existent* (completely independent), *immutable* (unchangeable), and *sovereign* (has unlimited authority), there is nothing we could ever need that cannot be found in Him!

Making God Happy

God has other attributes besides those we just mentioned—attributes that we share in (2 Peter 1:3-4, page 938). As we display them in our lives it brings great pleasure to Him.

Read Galatians 5:22-23 (page 893) and list the attributes.

1.

2.

3.

4.

5.

6.

7.

8.

9.

These are the traits (fruit) that God the Holy Spirit naturally produces in us. Now read the two following verses, 24 and 25.

What do we clear out of the way so God's traits (the fruit of the Spirit) are exhibited in us?

Sinful nature refers to the sin influence that remains with us after God's new creation has come and we have been born again into His new life. Many Bible translations use the term *flesh* instead of *sinful nature*. Galatians 5:16-17 (page 893) tells us that the sinful nature and the Holy Spirit in us are opposed to each other.

Verse 25 goes on to tell us something wonderful—that we as believers are living by the Spirit. Given this truth, how is your life different on a daily basis?

Displaying God's Character Traits

Let's look at each of these godly attributes (aspects of the fruit of the Spirit) and see how they can be shown in our lives.

Love. Read John 13:34-35 (page 823).

What does it say?

Our love for each other proves we are Jesus' disciples. Can you think of a recent circumstance when you exhibited such love? How do you think it might have influenced people around you?

Joy. Look at Philippians 4:4 (page 901).

What are some practical ways you can *"always be full of joy"*?

What in your life makes you *"full of joy"*?

"Always" is pretty all-encompassing, isn't it? How do you think you can let God's Spirit give you joy even in the dark moments of your life?

If we focus on our circumstances, it will be very difficult to exhibit joy. However, we can choose to stay in communion with our Sovereign God through the Holy Spirit in us. He knows about all our circumstances and has promised to walk through them with us. Then our lives will exude joy because we'll be experiencing God's presence with us and in us.

Peace. Read Philippians 4:6-7 (page 901).

What do these verses say we should worry about?

How do they describe the kind of peace God wants to give us?

What will that peace do?

Do you see the beautiful cycle this forms? God's gives us His peace ➔ it guards our hearts and minds ➔ that protects us from worry ➔ so we have His peace ➔ it guards our hearts and minds…Isn't God amazing?

Take a moment and reflect on these truths.

Patience. Now read Colossians 3:12-13 (page 903-904) and James 5:7-11 (page 932).

Patience always pays off. Can you think of a recent example of this in your life?

Kindness. Look at Ephesians 4:32 (page 897).

Do you find it interesting that kindness and forgiveness are tied together in this verse? Why do you think this is?

Goodness. Read Romans 14:17-19 (page 867) and 1 Peter 2:9 (page 935).

How do you define goodness? How does God show His goodness?

What do the verses in Romans associate goodness with? How would you exhibit this trait?

Faithfulness. Read Luke 16:9-12 (pages 798-799) and 3 John 3-4 (page 946).

Are there degrees of faithfulness?

What are your thoughts on the little things and large things the verses in Luke refer to?

What does the apostle John associate faithfulness with?

Gentleness. Read Titus 3:2 (page 918).

Why do you think slander and quarreling are mentioned before gentleness and humility?

When you show gentleness and humility, what do you look like to the people you interact with daily?

Self-control. Look at 1 Peter 1:13-14 (page 934).

In the Bible, self-control is linked to living in accord with who we are: *"God's obedient children,"* as the apostle Peter says. It means not slipping back into living only according to our own desires, the way we lived before Christ. We indulged in things like drunkenness and drugs, wild parties, out-of-bounds sex, overeating, envy, greed, hatred, uncontrolled anger and rage— a long, ugly list. None of these behaviors are consistent with our new life in Christ, and God is delighted when He sees us letting ourselves be controlled by the Holy Spirit instead of destructive behaviors and attitudes.

In what areas of your life do you see the Spirit developing more self-control?

Where do you see opportunities to grow by letting Him have more influence?

Displaying God's Holiness

Now go forward a couple of verses in 1 Peter 1. We discussed holiness quite a bit in chapter 2, and we saw God's wonderful plan to share His holiness with us. Read 1 Peter 1:15-16 (page 934).

The verses about holiness immediately follow those that talk about self-control. Why do you think this is?

Take a look at 1 Thessalonians 4:3-5 (page 906).

What is the contrast that is drawn between people in these verses?

One of the "loudest" witnesses to the fact that God exists is *us*. People look at our lives. They look at the attributes we exhibit, and are either drawn toward God or repelled. Behaving in a way that is holy does not mean perfection. Although we are in relationship with God, we still sometimes choose to follow the old ways of our sinful nature. But in our desire to be like the God we love—painting an accurate reflection of Him to the world around us—we will want to follow Him and listen to the Spirit more and more.

We Reflect God by Doing Things His Way

In the Bible, we see very clearly that doing things God's way is completely beneficial to us. Doing things His way is not a burdensome load of rules, principles, checklists, and guidelines that He imposes on us from outside (Matthew 11:28-30, page 742). Instead, He has written His law in our hearts (Hebrews 10:14-18, pages 925-926). It is now *natural* for us to want to live His way. Isn't that exciting and liberating?

God has changed our lives from the inside out. Deep inside us, He has given us the presence of the Holy Spirit, who changes the way we think as we allow Him to. God is *for* us! (Romans 8:28-32, page 863).

Isn't all of this a great thing to reveal about Him to those around us? Read the following verses, and note what characteristics our lives will exhibit as we follow His ways.

John 14:15 (page 823)

Romans 12:1-2 (page 866)

Remember the goal-weight analogy? As you invest in your relationship with God, as you stay close to His Word and follow Him,
your desire to listen to Him and obey Him keeps growing. The more
responsive and obedient you are, the more natural obedience becomes.
The difficulty comes when you try to live both the old way—the way
of the sinful nature—and God's way.

Which of the above verses represents your biggest challenge?

Let's look at some final verses about God's will and way. Read 1 Thessalonians 5:16-18 (page 907).

These verses are key to delighting our wonderful, generous God and walking in His ways. So how can we, in practical terms, be joyful and thankful no matter what?

What command was written between being joyful and being thankful (verse 17)?

How does being continually in touch with God through prayer play a part in your being joyful and thankful?

As you stay in touch with God, you will find yourself trusting Him and resting in His sovereignty *no matter what*. You will begin to exhibit both joy and gratitude. You see, joy and gratitude are *God's* attitudes. You will be changed as you spend time with Him. You will see His power released into your life, and all the other attitudes and behaviors God wants you to exhibit will start to be revealed. And your actions and attitudes will impact your personal sphere of influence. The people around you will watch how you face your challenges, and they will want to have that same loving, wonderful Person in their lives. You will become a mighty witness for God!

When You're Not Sure What God Would Like You to Do

When you are facing a decision and you're not sure what God would like you to do, talk to Him first. You need never fear approaching Him, because He is *for* you. It can also be helpful to prayerfully run your decision through this "question filter":

- Is there something in the Bible that indicates this action is inconsistent with the life I now live in Christ?
- If I do this, will it give God my Father pleasure?
- Will it help me—or hinder me —from growing closer to Him?
- Is this choice consistent with my love for Him?
- Will it show others that I love Him?
- Am I struggling to do things independently, or do I want to trust Him and rest in Him?

The answer to these questions will help you make the right decision. And just as in everything else, God is always there for you: That is just who He is. Read the following verses.

Psalm 25:4-5 (page 424)

Hebrews 13:5-6 (page 928)

God will take your hand. He will *never* abandon you. He is your Helper, and He will keep you on track!

Giving God Glory

Giving God glory is very closely connected to the two topics we've just discussed: making God happy and reflecting Him by doing things His way. When we live according to His ways, we give Him glory. When we show who He is and how wonderful He is through our lives and actions, we give Him glory. When we reveal the reality of His life working in our lives day by day, we give Him glory. When we speak highly of Him before other people and give Him honor for all the good in our lives, we give Him glory. It happens naturally as we stay close to Him and listen to Him.

"Giving glory" to someone is not something that happens much at all today. Maybe you are puzzled about the phrase. When we speak of giving glory to God, we mean that we are giving Him the credit for doing something in and through our lives. We're acknowledging that whatever good things "shine out" or radiate from us are really from Him and because of Him.

Now here is another amazing thing. God actually planned that we would *share* in the glory that He has always had. Read Romans 5:1-2 (page 860).

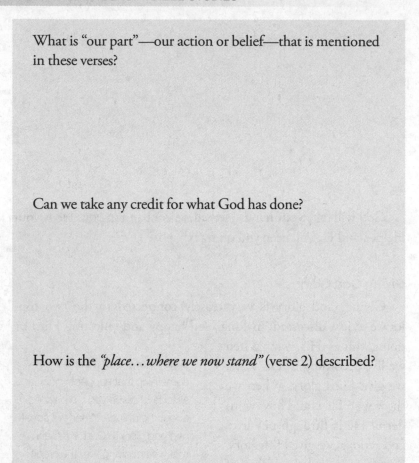

What is "our part"—our action or belief—that is mentioned in these verses?

Can we take any credit for what God has done?

How is the *place...where we now stand* (verse 2) described?

Whatever God has chosen to give to us and share with us is entirely out of His love, His initiative, and His generous heart. We have done—and need do—nothing to deserve it. Isn't that a great reason to give Him glory?

Our Attitude and Motivation

Key ways we give God glory are through our attitude and our motivation. These evidences of His Spirit in our lives make us living witnesses to His existence.

What do the following verses say about how we can bring Him glory?

John 15:5-8 (page 824)

1 Peter 4:10-11 (page 936)

Do you see the importance our attitude of dependence on God plays in glorifying Him? He is everything! Read the next verses and note who else is mentioned:

1 Corinthians 10:24,31-33 (page 876)

Colossians 3:22-24 (page 904)

Isn't it amazing? We don't give God glory by what we do so much as by our attitude toward those around us when we do it. Mopping the floor will give God glory, if our attitude is aligned with His! It's all about relationships!

What do you particularly not like to do? If you apply these verses to that chore or responsibility, how would you do it differently?

Read Romans 15:5-7 (page 868). How can you bring glory to God in other practical, relational ways?

God's Greatness Is Shown Through Our Weakness

The more we learn about God from the Bible, the more aware we are of His purity, holiness, righteousness, and wisdom. The closer we come to His light and love, the more clearly we see that apart from our connection with Him through Christ, we can do nothing (John 15:4-5, page 824). The more we depend on Him, the more Jesus can be seen in us!

When we admit our weaknesses—pride, the wish to be independent, the desire to control our own lives—God reveals His mighty strength in us. Read 2 Corinthians 12:9-10 (page 888).

Why did the apostle Paul actually *"take pleasure"* in his weaknesses?

Through our weakness, we become living displays of God's strength, and as that happens, we show forth who He is. We bring glory to Him!

We've almost come to the end of this study, but the question of our weakness and God's strength brings us to one final passage. When Jesus was living on this earth, He was constantly being questioned by the religious leaders. His answers often confused and angered them because it forced them to rethink their beliefs. They were always trying to trick Him. One day, one of them asked Jesus what was the most important of all the commandments. See how Jesus answered them in Mark 12:28-31 (page 773).

What did Jesus say is the most important commandment?

Think about those four areas for a minute: heart, soul, mind, and strength. Is there any area of human effort they don't cover? What do they signify to you?

Love God—with *all* your heart, *all* your soul, *all* your mind, *all* your strength. Consider it for a minute. Could there be a commandment more perfectly designed to expose every area of human weakness and incapability? Is there any way we could fulfill this apart from having God's own life in us through the Holy Spirit? And we do! That's a great reason to give Him glory, isn't it?

How do you think this commandment might "look" as the Holy Spirit expresses it through your attitudes and actions?

What does Jesus say is the second most important commandment?

What does *"love your neighbor as yourself"* look like as the Holy Spirit expresses it through you? In what areas of your behavior do you need to allow Him to better express Himself?

Some verses that might help with this are in Philippians 2:2-4 (page 900). What five characteristics will you display as you allow the Holy Spirit to control you?

1.

2.

3.

4.

5.

Do you want to bring God glory? Do you want to live an abundant life, beyond anything you ever imagined? Then *rest* in Him. *Rest* and trust in everything He has provided. Give up on trying to live independently. Thank Him for your weakness, the weakness that allows Him to show His mighty power through you.

Let *Him* be your abundance. Set your mind and heart on Him above all else. He will mold your attitudes and your behavior. You will know His love and friendship…and He will get the credit for everything.

> *All glory to God, who is able,*
> *through his mighty power at work within us,*
> *to accomplish infinitely more than we might ask or think.*
> —Ephesians 3:20 (page 896)

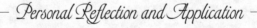

Personal Reflection and Application

From this chapter,

I see…

I believe…

I will…

Prayer

Father, I pray that my love will overflow more and more, and that I will keep on growing in knowledge and understanding. Help me to understand what really matters, so that I may live a pure and blameless life until Christ's return. Let me always be filled with the fruit of your salvation—the righteous character produced in me by Jesus Christ—so that I will bring much glory and praise to you (Philippians 1:9-11, page 899).

Thoughts, Notes, and Prayer Requests

_____

_____

_____

_____

_____

_____

_____

_____

_____

_____

_____

_____

_____

_____

Journal Pages

Know God

It does not matter what has happened in your past. No matter what you've done, no matter how you've lived your life,

God is personally interested in you right now.
He cares about you.

God understands your frustration, your loneliness, your heartaches. He wants each of us to come to Him, to know Him personally.

God is so rich in mercy, and he loved us so much, that even
though we were dead because of our sins, he gave us
life when he raised Christ from the dead.
(It is only by God's grace that you have been saved!)
—Ephesians 2:4-5 (page 895)

God loves you.

He created you in His image. His desire is to be in relationship with you. He wants you to belong to Him.

Sadly, our sin gets in the way. It separates us from God, and without Him we are dead in our spirits. There is nothing we can do to close that gap. There is nothing we can do to give ourselves life. No matter how well we may behave.

But God loves us so much He made a way to eliminate that gap and give us new life, His kind of life—to restore the relationship. His love for us is so great, so tremendous, that He sent Jesus Christ, His only Son, to earth to live, and then die—filling the gap and taking the punishment we deserve for refusing God's ways.

> God made Christ, who never sinned, to be the offering for our sin,
> so that we could be made right with God through Christ.
> —2 Corinthians 5:21 (page 884)

Jesus Christ, God's Son, not only died to pay the penalty for your sin, but He conquered death when He rose from the grave. He is ready to share His life with you.

Christ reconciles us to God. Jesus is alive today. He will give you a new beginning and a newly created life when you surrender control of your life to Him.

> Anyone who belongs to Christ has become a new person.
> The old life is gone; a new life has begun!
> —2 Corinthians 5:17 (page 884)

How do you begin this new life? You need to realize

> ...the necessity of repenting from sin and turning to God,
> and of having faith in our Lord Jesus.
> —Acts 20:21 (page 849)

Agree with God about your sins and believe that Jesus came to save you, that He is your Savior and Lord. Ask Him to lead your life.

God loved the world so much that he gave his one and only Son, so that everyone who believes in him will not perish but have eternal life. God sent his Son into the world not to judge the world, but to save the world through him.
—John 3:16-17 (page 811)

Pray something like this:

Jesus, I do believe you are the Son of God and that you died on the cross to pay the penalty for my sin. Forgive me. I turn away from sin and choose to live a life that pleases you. Enter my life as my Savior and Lord.

I want to follow you and make you the leader of my life.

Thank you for your gift of eternal life and for the Holy Spirit, who has now come to live in me. I ask this in your name. Amen.

God puts His Spirit inside you, who enables you to live a life pleasing to Him. He gives you new life that will never die, that will last forever—eternally.

When you surrender your life to Jesus Christ, you are making the most important decision of your life. Stonecroft would like to offer you a free download of *A New Beginning,* a short Bible study that will help you as you begin your new life in Christ. Go to **stonecroft.org/newbeginning**.

If you'd like to talk with someone right now about this prayer, call **1.888.NEED.HIM**.

Who Is Stonecroft?

Every day Stonecroft communicates the Gospel in meaningful ways. Whether side by side with a neighbor or new friend, or through a speaker sharing her transformational story, the Gospel of Jesus Christ goes forward. Through a variety of outreach activities and small group Bible studies specifically designed for those not familiar with God, and with online and print resources focused on evangelism, Stonecroft proclaims the Gospel of Jesus Christ to women where they are, as they are.

For more than 75 years, always with a foundation of prayer in reliance on God, Stonecroft volunteers have found ways to introduce women to Jesus Christ and train them to share His Good News with others.

Stonecroft understands and appreciates the influence of one woman's life. When you reach her, you touch everyone she knows—her family, friends, neighbors, and co-workers. The real Truth of the Gospel brings real redemption into real lives.

Our life-changing, faith-building community resources include:

- *Stonecroft Bible and Book Studies*—both topical and chapter-by-chapter studies. We designed Stonecroft studies for those in small groups—those who know Christ and those who do not yet know Him—to simply yet profoundly discover God's Word together.

- **Stonecroft Prays!**—calls small groups of women together to pray for God to show them avenues to reach women in their community with the Gospel.

- **Outreach Events**—set the stage for women to hear and share the Gospel with their communities. Whether in a large venue, workshop, or small group setting, Stonecroft women find ways to share the love of Christ.

- **Stonecroft Military**—a specialized effort to honor women connected to the U.S. military and share the Gospel with them while showing them the love of Christ.

- **Small Group Studies for Christians**—these resources reveal God's heart for those who do not yet know Him. The Aware Series includes *Aware*, *Belong*, and *Call*.

- **Stonecroft Life Publications**—clearly explain the Gospel through stories of people whose lives have been transformed by Jesus Christ.

- **Stonecroft.org**—offers fresh content daily to equip and encourage you.

Dedicated and enthusiastic Stonecroft staff serve you via Divisional Field Directors stationed across the United States, and a Home Office team who support tens of thousands of dedicated volunteers worldwide.

Your life matters. Join us today to impact your communities with the Gospel of Jesus Christ. Become involved with Stonecroft.

STONECROFT

Get started: connections@stonecroft.org 800.525.8627	Support Stonecroft: stonecroft.org/donate	Order resources: stonecroft.org/store 888.819.5218

Books for Further Study

Enns, Paul. *The Moody Handbook of Theology,* rev. ed. Chicago: Moody Publishers, 2008.

Ingram, Chip. *God: As He Longs for You to See Him.* Grand Rapids, MI: Baker Books, 2004.

Keller, Timothy. *The Prodigal God.* New York: Penguin Group, Inc., 2008.

McDowell, Josh. *New Evidence That Demands a Verdict.* Nashville, TN: Thomas Nelson, Inc., 1999.

Packer, J.I. *Knowing God.* Downers Grove, IL: InterVarsity Press, 1973, 1993.

Ryrie, Charles C. *Basic Theology: A Popular Systematic Guide to Understanding Biblical Truth.* Chicago: Moody Publishers, 1999.

Tozer, A.W. *The Knowledge of the Holy.* New York: HarperCollins Publishers, 1992.

Willmington, Harold L. *Willmington's Guide to the Bible,* rev. ed. Carol Stream, IL: Tyndale House Publishers, 2011.

Stonecroft Resources

Stonecroft Bible Studies make the Word of God accessible to everyone. These studies allow small groups to discover the adventure of a personal relationship with God and introduce others to God's unlimited love, grace, forgiveness, and power. To learn more, visit **stonecroft.org/biblestudies.**

Who Is Jesus? (6 chapters)
He was a rebel against the status quo. The religious community viewed Him as a threat. The helpless and outcast considered Him a friend. Explore the life and teachings of Jesus—this rebel with a cause who challenges us today to a life of radical faith.

What Is God Like? (6 chapters)
What is God like? Is He just a higher power? Has He created us and left us on our own? Where is He when things don't make sense? Discover what the Bible tells us about God and how we can know Him in a life-transforming way.

Who Is the Holy Spirit? (6 chapters)
Are you living up to the full life that God has for you? Learn about the Holy Spirit, our Helper and power source for everyday living, who works in perfect harmony with God the Father and Jesus the Son.

Connecting with God (8 chapters)
Prayer is our heart-to-heart communication with our heavenly Father. This study examines the purpose, power, and elements of prayer, sharing biblical principles for effective prayer.

Prayer Worth Repeating (15 devotions)

There is no place where your prayers to the one and only God cannot penetrate, no circumstance prayers cannot impact. As the mother of adult children, your greatest influence into their lives is through prayer. *Prayer Worth Repeating* is a devotional prayer guide designed to focus your prayers and encourage you to trust God more deeply as He works in the lives of your adult children.

Pray & Play Devotional (12 devotions)

It's playgroup with a purpose! Plus Mom tips. For details on starting a Pray & Play group, visit **stonecroft.org/prayandplay** or call **800.525.8627**.

Aware (5 lessons)

Making Jesus known every day starts when we are *Aware* of those around us. This dynamic Stonecroft Small Group Bible Study about "Always Watching and Responding with Encouragement" equips and engages people in the initial steps to the joys of evangelism.

Belong (6 lessons)

For many in today's culture, the desire to belong is often part of their journey to believe. *Belong* explores how we can follow in Jesus' footsteps—and walk with others on their journey to belong.

Call

Every day we meet people without Christ. That is God's intention. He wants His people to initiate and build friendships. He wants us together. *Call* helps us take a closer look at how God makes Himself known through our relationships with those around us.

Discover together God's clear calling for you and those near to you.